96 FACTS

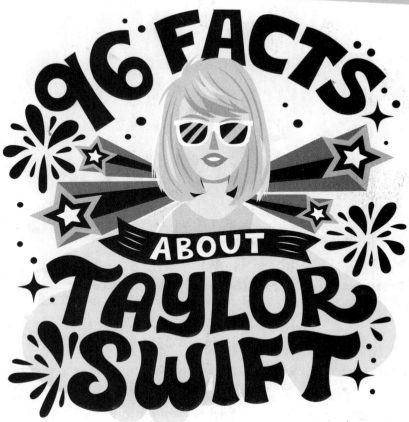

ABOUT
TAYLOR SWIFT

Quizzes, QUOTES, QUESTIONS, and MORE!

— BY ARIE KAPLAN —

ILLUSTRATED BY Risa Rodil

Grosset & Dunlap

GROSSET & DUNLAP
An imprint of Penguin Random House LLC, New York

First published in the United States of America by Grosset & Dunlap,
an imprint of Penguin Random House LLC, New York, 2023

Text copyright © 2023 by Arie Kaplan
Illustrations copyright © 2023 by Risa Rodil

Photo credits: 13, 29, 45, 61, 73: (speech bubbles with question marks)
Oleksandr Melnyk/iStock/Getty Images

GROSSET & DUNLAP is a registered trademark of
Penguin Random House LLC.

Visit us online at penguinrandomhouse.com.

Printed in the United States of America

ISBN 9780593750933   12   COMR

Design by Kimberley Sampson

TABLE OF CONTENTS

Part I

THE EARLY YEARS: CHRISTMAS TREES AND LEANN RIMES CDS
America's Sweetheart

She's the total package. A vocalist of astounding power and gravitas. A talented songwriter with a diverse range, she can create mature, thoughtful compositions as well as light, frothy pop hits. She's Taylor Swift. Often referred to as "America's Sweetheart," she's actually so much more than that.

Maybe you like her early country music songs or her more experimental albums like *Folklore*. Perhaps you dance to "Shake It Off" when you need to de-stress after a tough day at school.

But who is Taylor Swift, and how did she get to be one of the most iconic stars in the history of popular music? Believe it or not, before all the glitz and the glamour, she was just a small child with big dreams.

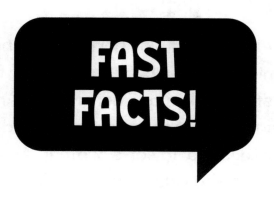

FAST FACTS!

While she's adept at playing the piano, banjo, and ukulele, Taylor prefers playing the guitar.

Taylor Swift was named after singer and songwriter James Taylor, one of her parents' favorite artists.

A Magical Childhood

Taylor Alison Swift was born in Reading, Pennsylvania, on December 13, 1989. Her father, Scott, is a stockbroker, and her mother, Andrea, is a homemaker and a former mutual fund marketing executive. Taylor's brother, Austin, was born when she was two years old.

Taylor's childhood was, in some ways, like something out of a fairy tale. She grew up on her parents' Christmas tree farm in Reading, where she rode horses and enjoyed the wide-open spaces.

But in certain ways, Taylor had a childhood like any other. True, she was surrounded by Christmas trees and ponies for the first decade of her life. But like any other kid, she had to help out around the house. At the farm, this meant that it was her job to pick praying mantis pods off the trees before they were sold to customers.

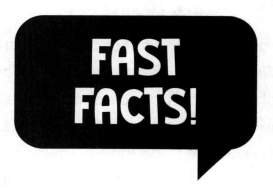

FAST FACTS!

In 2019, Taylor Swift released a song called "Christmas Tree Farm," which was inspired by her childhood.

Taylor Swift believes that thirteen is her lucky number. She was born on December 13, her first album went gold in thirteen weeks, and her first single, "Tim McGraw," had a thirteen-second intro.

The New Kid in Town

When Taylor was in fifth grade, her family moved to Wyomissing, Pennsylvania. Because of the move, she had to change schools. She didn't know anyone at her new school in Wyomissing, and she felt awkward and lonely. Taylor was searching for something that made her feel seen. She found that "something" in country music. She was a big fan of many strong, charismatic female performers in the country music world, such as the Chicks, Shania Twain, and LeAnn Rimes.

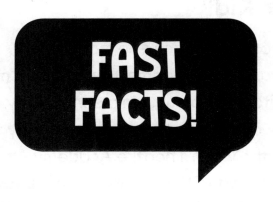

FAST FACTS!

LeAnn Rimes was Taylor Swift's hero when she was growing up. Taylor got her first LeAnn Rimes CD when she was six years old.

Taylor won a national poetry contest after she moved to Wyomissing. Her winning entry was a poem called "There's a Monster in My Closet."

Theater Kid

Also around the time she moved to Wyomissing, Taylor became interested in musical theater. After performing in a school play, she began appearing in musicals produced by the Berks County Youth Theatre Academy.

When she wasn't acting in musicals, Taylor tried singing like her country music idols. She soon realized that she liked singing more than acting. Since LeAnn Rimes started her career at age thirteen, Taylor thought she'd do that as well. After all, Taylor was eleven, which was *almost* thirteen!

FAST FACTS!

While Taylor was a member of Berks County Youth Theatre Academy, she also enjoyed performing karaoke. In fact, she entered karaoke competitions every week!

During this period, Taylor had an acting coach who believed in her so much, he rented space in a local mall just so Taylor could perform there, belting country songs to karaoke backing tracks.

Did You Know That . . .

1 Taylor's parents gave her a gender-neutral first name so that if someone saw her name on a business résumé when she was an adult, they wouldn't judge her based on gender bias.

2 Taylor's zodiac sign is Sagittarius.

3 Taylor's ancestry includes Scottish, Welsh, English, German, Irish, and a bit of Italian.

4 Taylor's parents, Scott Swift and Andrea Gardner Swift, first met when Scott was on a business trip in Andrea's hometown of Harris County, Texas.

5 Taylor's parents were married on February 20, 1988, in Houston, Texas.

6 Taylor's parents' Christmas tree farm was eleven acres wide.

7 The Christmas tree farm was located in rural Cumru Township, in Reading, Pennsylvania.

8 Taylor's brother's full name is Austin Kingsley Swift.

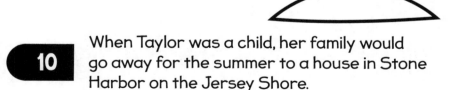

9 Austin was born on March 11, 1992.

10 When Taylor was a child, her family would go away for the summer to a house in Stone Harbor on the Jersey Shore.

Thank-You Notes

"I love writing thank-you notes. There's something very nostalgic to me about the feel of a card and putting pen to paper."

—Taylor on writing thank-you cards

If you were to write a thank-you note, who would you write it to? A family member? Your best friend? A teacher? On the lines below, write a thank-you note to the person who's helped you the most during the past year.

_____

_____

_____

_____

_____

_____

_____

_____

_____

_____

_____

_____

_____

_____

_____

_____

_____

_____

_____

Trying New Things

When Taylor moved to Wyomissing, Pennsylvania, she didn't know anyone there. It was a new town and a new experience for her. Have you ever tried to do something you've never done before? Have you ever moved somewhere new, either temporarily or permanently? What was that experience like?

_____

_____

_____

_____

_____

_____

_____

_____

_____

_____

_____

_____

_____

_____

_____

_____

Quick Quiz: A Swift Childhood

1) **What did Taylor's maternal grandmother, Marjorie Finlay, do for a living?**

    a. She was a vampire hunter.
    b. She was an opera singer.
    c. She was an underwater ventriloquist.
    d. She was a turnip collector.

2) **Which famous pop group did Taylor listen to as a preteen?**

    a. Alvin and the Chipmunks
    b. Dr. Teeth and the Electric Mayhem
    c. Josie and the Pussycats
    d. The Backstreet Boys

3) **What grade was Taylor in when she won a national poetry contest for her "Monster in My Closet" poem?**

    a. Pre-K
    b. First
    c. Fifth
    d. Kindergarten

4) **The music video for Taylor's song "Christmas Tree Farm" includes what?**

    a. Footage from home movies shot by Taylor's parents

    b. A cameo by Frosty the Snowman

    c. A scene where Godzilla decorates an enormous Christmas tree

    d. Deleted scenes from the film *The Nightmare Before Christmas*

5) **What private school did Taylor attend until she was nine years old?**

    a. Nevermore Academy

    b. The Wyndcroft School

    c. Xavier's School for Gifted Youngsters

    d. Hogwarts

Check your answers on page 78!

Part II

RISE TO FAME: LEARNING THE ROPES
Destination: Nashville

When Taylor Swift was eleven years old, she decided to officially begin pursuing a career as a professional singer. One day, she saw a Faith Hill television special in which the singer spoke about hitting it big in Nashville, Tennessee. From then on, this was Taylor's goal: to make it in Nashville, the country music capital of America.

So Taylor spent her spring break taking a road trip to Nashville with her mom. The two of them visited the offices of over twenty record companies and gave out copies of Taylor's demo tape. One record executive gave her good advice: Stop recording covers of other people's tunes. Instead, sing your own original songs. It was advice that changed Taylor's life. Now she would focus on what she had to say as an artist, instead of imitating her musical heroes.

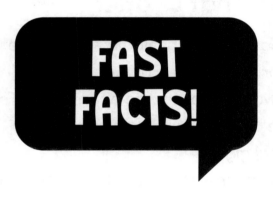

FAST FACTS!

When Taylor and her mom took that spring break road trip to Nashville, they had Taylor's little brother, Austin, in the back seat.

These days, Austin Swift is an actor who also manages his sister's film projects.

Climbing That Ladder

When Taylor was in middle school, she won a karaoke contest at the Pat Garrett Roadhouse. The prize was a spot as the opening act for the Charlie Daniels Band. It was her first professional gig!

Shortly afterward, her parents moved the family to Hendersonville, Tennessee, so that Taylor could be closer to Nashville. That way, it would be easier for her to pursue her musical dreams.

Soon, the fourteen-year-old singer was signed to an artist development deal at a popular record label called RCA. She also had an original track featured on a Maybelline compilation album called *Chicks with Attitude*, and she appeared in an Abercrombie & Fitch "Rising Stars" ad campaign. Which is appropriate since Taylor was indeed a rising star!

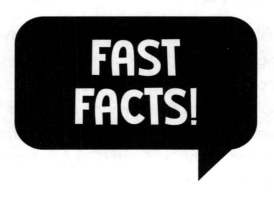

FAST FACTS!

An artist development deal is what a record label offers a recording artist when they don't feel ready to commit to a record deal. So they spend time mentoring the artist and developing the early stages of their career.

Hendersonville is also where Taylor met her friend Abigail Anderson, who is name-checked in Taylor's 2008 song "Fifteen."

On Her Own

By age fifteen, Taylor had written over two hundred original songs. But RCA still wouldn't sign her to a record contract. However, RCA *did* set up after-school songwriting sessions for Taylor, where she was mentored by experienced tunesmiths like Liz Rose. Taylor and Liz hit it off, and Taylor appreciated the advice Liz gave her.

RCA told Taylor that she would be kept in development and wouldn't be signed to a record deal until she was eighteen. So Taylor walked away from the development deal. In the music industry, you're not supposed to do that unless you have another record label to go to. But Taylor wasn't getting anywhere at RCA.

One night in 2005, Liz Rose invited Taylor to sing at the Bluebird Café in Nashville.

Entertainment industry executive Scott Borchetta was in the audience, and he was very impressed with Taylor. Months later, when Scott founded Big Machine Records, he signed her to a record deal. It was finally happening. Taylor Swift was going to make an album!

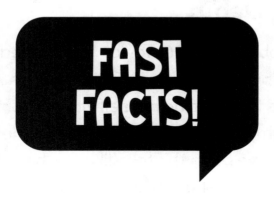

FAST FACTS!

In May 2004, music publishing company Sony/ATV Tree signed Taylor as a songwriter to pen songs for other recording artists. At fourteen years old, she was the youngest songwriter they'd ever signed!

In 2004 and 2005, when she was an emerging artist in the music world, Taylor was still a high-school student. Two subjects she excelled in were science and English.

Her Big Debut

In October of 2006, Taylor Swift released her first album. She called it *Taylor Swift*. After all, she was introducing herself to the world. People might as well get to know her name! Taylor might not have been thirteen like her hero LeAnn Rimes was when she made *her* debut. But Taylor was only sixteen, she was still in high school, and she had an album full of original songs under her belt. Not too shabby.

Taylor didn't have to wait long for the album to make an impression. *Taylor Swift* stayed on the *Billboard* 200 chart for 277 weeks straight. And "Tim McGraw," the first single released off the album, reached the top ten on *Billboard*'s Hot Country Songs.

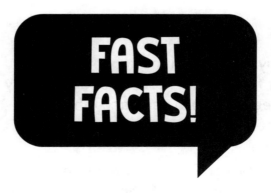

FAST FACTS!

One of the songs on *Taylor Swift* (titled "Our Song") is a tune Taylor originally wrote for her high-school talent show.

All five of the singles from Taylor's first album have been certified platinum or multiplatinum.

Did You Know That . . .

1 Taylor entered the karaoke contest at the Pat Garrett Roadhouse every weekend *for a year and a half* until she won.

2 In April of 2002, a twelve-year-old Taylor Swift sang "The Star-Spangled Banner" in front of twenty thousand people at the Philadelphia 76ers NBA Finals game.

3 Around the time Taylor moved to Hendersonville, her parents helped her get an agent named Dan Dymtrow.

4 Dan Dymtrow helped Taylor get meetings with big record executives.

5 Because she'd written "Our Song" for her high-school talent show, Taylor originally wasn't even going to put the song on her first album. Good thing she reconsidered!

6 Taylor's songwriting mentor Liz Rose was her writing partner for some of the songs on *Taylor Swift*.

7 "Tim McGraw" was one of those songs.

8 "Tim McGraw" is about a woman who's broken up with her boyfriend, and her best memories of their relationship are tied to a Tim McGraw song they used to listen to together.

9 The specific Tim McGraw song Taylor referenced in "Tim McGraw" is "Can't Tell Me Nothin'," from the iconic country star's *Live Like You Were Dying* album.

10 Taylor's debut album sold thirty-nine thousand copies in its first week.

Treating People Well

"I've never been more proud to have come from a community that's so rooted in songwriting, so rooted in hard work and in treating people well."

—Taylor's thoughts on Nashville, where she wrote many songs during her early career

When you hear the phrase "treating people well," what does that mean to you?

_____

_____

_____

_____

_____

_____

_____

_____

_____

_____

_____

_____

_____

_____

_____

_____

_____

_____

Role Models

When Taylor was growing up, she thought of LeAnn Rimes as a role model. Who is *your* role model? Your role model could be someone in your family or your community. They could also be an artist, celebrity, athlete, or activist you admire. Write about your role model on the lines below.

_____

_____

_____

_____

_____

_____

_____

_____

_____

_____

_____

_____

_____

_____

Quick Quiz: Taylor Finds Fame

1) When Taylor performed at the Bluebird Café that fateful night in 2005, which musical instrument did she play?

   a. The guitar
   b. The tuba
   c. The xylophone
   d. The cowbell

2) How long did it take Taylor Swift and Liz Rose to write the hit song "Tim McGraw"?

   a. Two hours
   b. Six hours
   c. Three hours
   d. Fifteen minutes

3) The song "Stay Beautiful," from Taylor's debut album, is about a girl who has a crush on a boy who moves away before she can tell him how she feels about him. What is that boy's name?

   a. Raphael
   b. Leonardo
   c. Cory
   d. Michelangelo

4) What was the original title for "Mary's Song"?

a. "Last Friday Night"
b. "Oh My My My"
c. "Firework"
d. "Teenage Dream"

5) Taylor Swift fans are called:

a. The Beyhive
b. Beliebers
c. Swifties
d. Little Monsters

Check your answers on page 78!

Part III

DEFINING MOMENTS, FROM *FEARLESS* TO *FOLKLORE*

Taylor Gets Fearless

Taylor Swift's career has progressed in phases, each of which signify that she's about to pivot artistically. For instance, her second studio album, *Fearless*, was released in the United States in November of 2008. The theme of the album was high-school romance, a subject her target audience knew all too well.

The first single from that album, "Love Story," sold over eighteen million copies, making it one of the best-selling singles of all time. The song is a riff on the William Shakespeare play *Romeo and Juliet*, about a forbidden love affair. Taylor was beginning to spread her wings—she was taking cues from classic literature and embracing different musical genres.

This was equally true in her third album, *Speak Now*, which came out in 2010, when Taylor was twenty years old. This album had a country sound, no doubt. But a fan with a keen ear would notice that Taylor was pivoting more toward pop music.

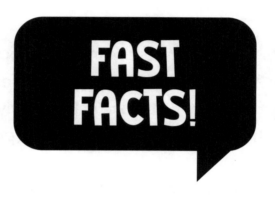

FAST FACTS!

"Love Story" went on to become the first song to hit number one on *Billboard*'s Top Country *and* Pop charts.

Speak Now signaled a shift in Taylor's songwriting style—her songs were becoming more *personal*.

Seeing Red

Taylor's fourth studio album, *Red*, dropped in October 2012. For many fans, this is the classic Taylor album. But more importantly, *Red* catapulted her into the mainstream pop stratosphere.

The album made naysayers take Taylor more seriously, because it marked a transition from songs about silly high-school crushes to more thoughtful, contemplative songs about painful subjects, like falling out of love with someone. This made sense, because Taylor was twenty-two years old now, and she could look at relationships through a more mature lens.

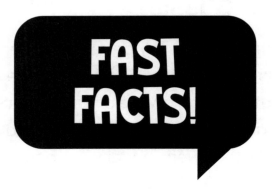

FAST FACTS!

Red's lead single, "We Are Never Ever Getting Back Together," was Taylor's first song to reach number one on the *Billboard* Hot 100.

The third single from *Red*, "I Knew You Were Trouble," was a look back at a toxic relationship. This song showed how Taylor had grown and changed as an artist.

Fame and Gossip

In November 2017, Taylor released her sixth studio album, *Reputation*. She wanted the world to know that she was aware of the rumors circulating around her in the press due to certain media outlets that were hungry for gossip about her personal life. And she didn't care what people were saying.

And as if the message of the album wasn't crystal clear, the music video for the album's most lead single, "Look What You Made Me Do," included a prominent image of Taylor's tombstone with the words "Here Lies Taylor Swift's Reputation" written on it. During the video, a zombie Taylor is seen emerging from the grave. The message is simple: Taylor has been reborn.

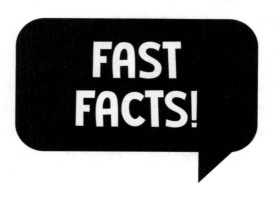

FAST FACTS!

Taylor announced *Reputation* by deleting all her old posts on social media and replacing them with a video of a hissing snake (a reference to the fact that some misinformed, gossipy folks thought of her as a "lying snake").

The fact that Taylor titled this album *Reputation* means that she was fully aware of how she was being perceived by the public. She wanted the album to shake up people's preconceived notions about her.

Surprise, Surprise

Most of the songs on Taylor's first seven albums were inspired by a real person, place, or thing that had a huge impact on her life. They were at least *semi*-autobiographical. Not so for her eighth album, *Folklore*, which was composed of songs about completely fictional characters and events.

Another way in which *Folklore* was a departure is that it was a "surprise" album; its very existence was a secret until Taylor unexpectedly released it with no advance publicity in July of 2020, during the (relatively) early days of the COVID-19 pandemic.

The same was true of her ninth album, *Evermore*, also a surprise release. *Evermore* dropped in December of 2020, a mere five months after *Folklore*. This meant Taylor Swift wrote both albums back-to-back, without taking a break, working remotely with producers and studio musicians, in the middle of a global pandemic. Wow. You've got to respect that work ethic!

FAST FACTS!

In 2020, Taylor won the Songwriter of the Year award from Apple Music for *Folklore*.

The songs for *Folklore* are often considered an example of "cottagecore," a style of art and music that celebrates an idealized rural life of cozy farmhouses and tranquil forests.

1 Taylor devised the song "Fearless" (from the album of the same name) while touring as an opening act for other musicians.

2 "Fearless" (the song, not the album) is about Taylor's idea of what the perfect first date might be like.

3 In 2009, *Fearless* won the Grammy for Album of the Year.

4 After the release of *Fearless*, each of her next three albums (*Speak Now*, *Red*, and *1989*) went platinum in their first week.

5 Taylor plays *both* of the female leads in the music video for the song "You Belong with Me."

6 *Speak Now* was the first album on which Taylor Swift wrote all the songs herself, without any help from cowriters like Liz Rose.

7 Taylor contributed two songs to the soundtrack of the 2012 film *The Hunger Games*: the solo effort "Eyes Open" and "Safe & Sound" (a collaboration with the alternative country duo The Civil Wars).

8 *Red*'s lead single, "We Are Never Ever Getting Back Together," was written by Taylor Swift, Max Martin, and Shellback.

9 Max Martin is a Swedish songwriter and music producer who has crafted hit singles for many pop stars, including Britney Spears's "...Baby One More Time" (1998), and NSYNC's "It's Gonna Be Me" (2000).

10 In 2014, *Red* earned four nominations at the 56th Annual Grammy Awards.

Overcoming Your Fear

"I guess, to me, fearless doesn't mean you're completely unafraid and it doesn't mean that you're bulletproof. It means that you have a lot of fears, but you jump anyway."

—Taylor on being fearless

Have you ever been afraid of something, but you did it, anyway? What was that like? Write about it on the lines below.

_____

_____

_____

_____

_____

_____

_____

_____

_____

_____

_____

_____

_____

_____

_____

_____

_____

_____

_____

_____

Rude Rumors

Taylor wrote some of the songs on her *Reputation* album because she wanted people to know she didn't like the rumors that were being spread about her. Has anyone ever spread a rumor about you, or about someone you know?

Did you tell your parents or grown-ups, or your friends? What advice did they give you?

_____

_____

_____

_____

_____

_____

_____

_____

_____

_____

_____

_____

_____

_____

_____

_____

_____

_____

Quick Quiz: Complete the Lyric

As a Taylor Swift fan, you know the words to every one of her songs, right? Let's see just how well you know them! Fill in the blanks below to complete these Taylor Swift song lyrics:

1) **"I think I've seen this film before, and I didn't like the ____"**

   a. acting
   b. dialogue
   c. special effects
   d. ending

2) **"I remember when we ____ up the first time"**

   a. broke
   b. swam
   c. drove
   d. flew

3) **"I stay out too late, got nothing in my ____"**

   a. refrigerator
   b. wallet
   c. brain
   d. closet

4) "Cause ____, now we got bad blood, you know it used to be mad love"

   a. Shaggy
   b. baby
   c. Scooby
   d. Velma

5) "We could leave the ____ lights up 'til January"

   a. Christmas
   b. traffic
   c. spaceship
   d. lamppost

Check your answers on page 78!

Part IV

THE PUBLIC LIFE OF A VERY PRIVATE PERSON

Under a Microscope

As a public figure, Taylor Swift is constantly under a microscope. Not only have her songs and lyrics been the subject of critical analysis, but every aspect of her personal life has been dissected and commented upon. In short: There's a reason Taylor made an entire album (*Reputation*) about the toxicity of gossip and fame.

But instead of dwelling on that, it's better to look at the ways in which Taylor has helped people, and the friends who give her strength and support. You know, the positive stuff. The stuff that *won't* make it into an album like *Reputation*.

FAST FACTS!

When Taylor moved to New York City and began writing the songs for her album *1989*, she hosted get-togethers with friends at her apartment on Cornelia Street.

From 2013 to 2016, Taylor hosted elaborate Fourth of July parties, which sometimes included an inflatable slide and fireworks!

Giving Back

Taylor Swift is known for her talent. But she's also known for her selflessness. Family friends attribute Taylor's generosity and kindness to the values her parents instilled in her.

Throughout Taylor's career, she's shown a continued commitment to those values. In January 2010, she took part in *Hope for Haiti Now*, a charity telethon organized to benefit victims of the devastating earthquake that had struck Haiti the week before. She's continued her charity work in the years since. In 2015, after recording the single "Welcome to New York" (from the album *1989*), Taylor donated $50,000 in song proceeds to New York City schools. And in 2020, Taylor donated stimulus checks to several fans in order to help them get through the COVID-19 pandemic.

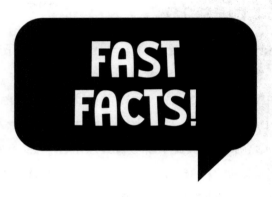

FAST FACTS!

It's no wonder Taylor wanted to help out New York City in 2015. She felt a kinship to the city after moving there the previous year to work on her album *1989*.

In 2020, in the wake of the George Floyd protests, Taylor showed solidarity with the protestors by donating to the NAACP Legal Defense Fund.

Faithful Friends

Ever since she dropped her first album, Taylor Swift's private life has been the focus of intense public scrutiny. Who is she dating? Did she just break up with her boyfriend? It often seems that everyone has an opinion about Taylor's personal life, even though it's just that: *her* personal life. In other words, it's her business *and nobody else*'s.

Because of that, one of the ways Taylor stays grounded is by having a close circle of friends she can count on when she needs to de-stress, vent, or simply celebrate her personal triumphs.

Some of her friends are famous themselves. Take model Gigi Hadid, one of Taylor's besties since 2015. They've gone to the beach together, acted together in the video for Taylor's "Bad Blood" music video, and dressed up together for Taylor's Halloween party.

Then there's Ed Sheeran. For over a decade, Ed and Taylor have stood by each other's side, whether performing duets together or just clowning around on social media.

FAST FACTS!

In the "Bad Blood" music video, Taylor plays a secret agent whose code name is Catastrophe, and Gigi plays her fellow agent, Slay-Z.

Taylor Swift and Ed Sheeran became friends in 2012, after Ed found out that Taylor wrote some of his lyrics on her arm during a show in Australia.

Live and in Concert

Songs are meant to be heard. But performances are meant to be *seen*. And Taylor's concert tours are a feast for the eyes.

During her *Fearless* tour in 2009, she went through multiple costume changes and performed in front of a set resembling a fairy-tale castle.

Two years later, the *Speak Now* tour had it all: Plumes of smoke! Fireworks! Circus-style aerialists flying through the air! A stage decorated like a theater from a bygone era!

Taylor's *Reputation* tour in 2018 involved enormous inflatable snakes and traveling cages that took Taylor from one part of the stage to the next.

All these concerts have one thing in common: Taylor wants everyone who sees her live to come away feeling that they've gotten their money's worth . . . and then some.

FAST FACTS!

During certain US dates in the *1989* tour (which happened in 2015), Taylor surprised the crowd by pointing out special guests in the audience, including John Legend, Avril Lavigne, and Mick Jagger. Many of these guests ran up onstage and performed with Taylor!

The day before the *Reputation* tour began in 2018, Taylor invited two thousand adopted and foster children to a two-hour private dress rehearsal!

1 Taylor and Gigi Hadid were first photographed together at an Oscars after-party in 2014. That's when the general public first realized that they were friends.

2 Taylor Swift and Ed Sheeran cowrote the song "Everything Has Changed," which appeared on Taylor's 2012 album, *Red*.

3 During one performance on the *Red* tour, Ed Sheeran came out onstage wearing a wool cap that resembled the internet sensation Grumpy Cat.

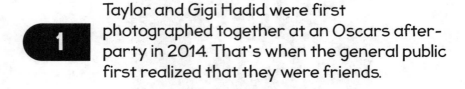

4 At Madison Square Garden in 2011, Taylor performed with her namesake, James Taylor.

5 She only performed two shows at Madison Square Garden that year, and both were sold-out.

6 Taylor Swift also mentioned James Taylor in her song "Begin Again."

7 In 2013, Taylor came out to cheer on Ed Sheeran during his own performance at Madison Square Garden. They sang "Everything Has Changed" together during the show.

8 Katy Perry and Taylor Swift dressed up as a burger and fries (respectively) for Taylor's "You Need to Calm Down" music video in 2019.

9 In 2015, Gigi Hadid and model Martha Hunt joined Taylor onstage during a concert in Detroit. As Taylor performed the song "Style," all three of them strutted their stuff, showing off their runway walk.

10 At Taylor Swift's Halloween party in 2016, Taylor dressed up as the Marvel superhero Deadpool, and Gigi Hadid dressed up as a Cub Scout.

Capture the Moment

"In this moment now— capture it, remember it."

—Taylor in her 2008 song "Fearless"

What's a special moment in your life that you'll always want to remember? Write about it on the lines below.

_____

_____

_____

_____

_____

_____

_____

_____

_____

_____

_____

_____

_____

_____

_____

_____

_____

_____

_____

_____

_____

Loyal Besties

Over the years, Taylor's friends Gigi Hadid and Ed Sheeran have been there for her whenever she needed someone to talk to. Who are your best friends? Write about them on the lines below.

_____

_____

_____

_____

_____

_____

_____

_____

_____

_____

_____

_____

_____

_____

_____

_____

_____

_____

Quick Quiz: Match the Performer to Their "Bad Blood" Character

Can you match the performer to the character they play in the "Bad Blood" music video?

PERFORMERS

A Jessica Alba

B Hailee Steinfeld

C Karlie Kloss

D Selena Gomez

E Kendrick Lamar

CHARACTER NAMES

Arsyn **1**

Knockout **2**

Welvin Da Great **3**

The Trinity **4**

Domino **5**

Check your answers on page 78!

Part V

WHAT'S NEXT FOR THE RENAISSANCE WOMAN?

Live from New York

Taylor Swift isn't *just* an award-winning recording artist and songwriter. Not that that isn't impressive enough (because it is), but she has other talents and interests beyond music. You might say she's a renaissance woman. That means that she's good at many different things.

For example, did you know that Taylor is hilariously funny? In 2009, she hosted the legendary sketch comedy series *Saturday Night Live*, and she crushed it! She was even the first host to write their own monologue! Usually, *SNL*'s staff writers craft the host's monologue, but Taylor penned and performed a tune called "My Monologue Song," which got huge laughs!

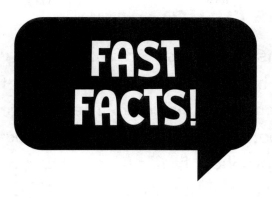

FAST FACTS!

Taylor doesn't just act in comedies. In 2009, before she hosted *SNL*, Taylor made her television acting debut as a rebellious teenager in an episode of the drama series *CSI: Crime Scene Investigation*.

Taylor has also appeared in several movies. In 2010, Taylor made her film acting debut in the romantic comedy *Valentine's Day*.

Fearless Future

Taylor is also a talented filmmaker. In recent years, she has directed the music videos for some of her songs, including "The Man" and "Willow" (both in 2020). In 2021, she directed *All Too Well: The Short Film*, a fifteen-minute-long film adaptation of her 2012 song "All Too Well."

What does the future hold for Taylor Swift? It's difficult to say. That's because part of Taylor's appeal is her unpredictability. Just when you think you understand what sort of artist she is—a country singer—she pivots and embraces other musical genres. Just when you think you understand the content of her songs—teen love ballads—she shifts gears and becomes a more complex, mature songwriter. So whatever she's got planned for the future, it'll be something totally surprising yet appropriately dazzling.

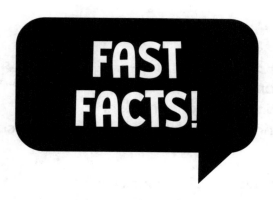

FAST FACTS!

All Too Well: The Short Film opens with the following quote from Chilean poet Pablo Neruda: "Love is so short, forgetting is so long."

In December of 2022, *Variety* reported that Taylor had signed a deal to write and direct a full-length feature film for Searchlight Pictures. No other details were available at the time, making this a very exciting and mysterious new project for Taylor!

Did You Know That . . .

1 In 2019, Taylor played Bombalurina in the film adaptation of composer Andrew Lloyd Webber's stage musical *Cats*.

2 In May 2022, Taylor Swift gave a commencement speech at New York University (also known as NYU).

3 Taylor also received an honorary doctorate from NYU.

4 Taylor owns her own jet plane.

5 Taylor is known for doing "meet-and-greets" where she meets some of her fans, both before and after her concerts.

6 As of this writing, Taylor has won three Grammy Awards for Album of the Year.

7 She has won twelve Grammy Awards in total.

8 *All Too Well: The Short Film* starred *Stranger Things* actor Sadie Sink and *Teen Wolf* actor Dylan O'Brien.

9 Taylor is the only solo artist who has won two Best Direction awards at the MTV Video Music Awards (also known as the VMAs).

10 She won those two Best Direction VMAs for *All Too Well: The Short Film* and the music video for "The Man."

The Soundtrack of Your Life

"I've always felt music is the only way to give an instantaneous moment the feel of slow motion. To romanticize it and glorify it and give it a soundtrack and a rhythm."

—Taylor on music

Have you ever thought about writing a song about your own personal experiences?

What is something that's happened to you that you feel would make a great song?

_____

_____

_____

_____

_____

_____

_____

_____

_____

_____

_____

_____

_____

_____

_____

_____

_____

Funny Stuff

Taylor Swift is very funny. She likes clowning around with her friends, and she likes acting in comedic television shows and movies. What's the funniest thing that has ever happened to you?

_____
_____
_____
_____
_____
_____
_____
_____
_____
_____
_____
_____
_____
_____
_____
_____
_____
_____

ANSWER KEY
Pages 18–19:
1) b, 2) d, 3) c, 4) a, 5) b

Pages 34–35:
1) a, 2) d, 3) c, 4) b, 5) c

Pages 50–51:
1) d, 2) a, 3) c, 4) b, 5) a

Pages 66–67:
A:5, B:4, C:2, D:1, E:3

ABOUT THE AUTHOR

Arie Kaplan began his career writing about pop music for magazines such as *Teen Beat*, *Tiger Beat*, and *BOP*. And over the years, he has satirized pop music as a writer for *MAD Magazine*. Arie is also the author of the juvenile nonfiction book *American Pop: Hit Makers, Superstars, and Dance Revolutionaries*.

As a nonfiction author, Arie is perhaps most well-known for the acclaimed book *From Krakow to Krypton: Jews and Comic Books*, a 2008 finalist for the National Jewish Book Award. He has also penned numerous books and graphic novels for young readers, including *LEGO Star Wars: The Official Stormtrooper Training Manual*, *The New Kid from Planet Glorf*, *Jurassic Park Little Golden Book*, *Frankie and the Dragon*, and *Swashbuckling Scoundrels: Pirates in Fact and Fiction*. Aside from his work as an author, Arie is a screenwriter for television, video games, and transmedia. Please check out his website: www.ariekaplan.com.